How Shared Leadership Is Created
and What Its Requirements Are

COMMUNITY-LED LEADERSHIP

KARL-JOHAN SPIIK

How Shared Leadership Is Created
and What Its Requirements Are

COMMUNITY-LED LEADERSHIP

KARLEX

2023

Karl-Johan Spiik

Leadership hacker:
a consultant for coaching-oriented
leadership and teamwork

Blog
www.spiik.net

Home page of the company
www.karlex.fi

**The measurements for
community-led methods**
www.yhteisöohjautuvuus.fi

The first book in this series
Community-Led Team

Additional information
www.yhdessaohjautuvatiimi.fi

Publisher: Karlex Oy
Layout and design: Eve Sillanpää

ISBN 978-952-65337-0-4 (softcover)
ISBN 978-952-65337-1-1 (PDF)
ISBN 978-952-65337-2-8 (MP3)

Print: BoD – Books on Demand, Norderstedt, Saksa

CONTENTS

1 FOREWORD

During my work career, I have worked for almost two decades with shared leadership. I have operated in small and big organizations and experienced many types of leadership. I have participated more than 60 projects with teams of different sizes. I have experienced projects with teams and people from many different organizations. In all of them the same guidelines have come up. Communication and shared practices stands as a cornerstone.

I have already as a young student studied the literature on agile project methods thoroughly. Different task lists, rotating roles, and dispersed decision making have been part of my everyday life throughout my career. At first I did not see that it was about different levels of leadership. I felt that it was just a typical model for the expert industry. As a result of the development of the community-led theories I have come to understand why the fields of technological expertise have been the forerunners in shared leadership.

The present information and communication technology enables sharing leadership. People do not need to be physically in the same space. They do not even have to work at the same time. The traditional model – where one supervises the others and manages the big picture – is unnecessary. Before, it was the forerunners of technology and those using it who in particular were well-versed in the tools of shared leadership. Now information technology is necessary everywhere, and the advanced methods of leadership can take over other fields, too.

Alongside the widespread use of information technology, people's emotional intelligence has a greater role today than before. In the traditional leadership model, the authority comes from above and anything coming from there is tolerated – sometimes even bullying and sexual harassment. Nowadays, respecting the boundaries and feelings of everyone is raised so high up as a value, that hierarchical models are no longer needed in organizations. Conflicts cannot be avoided, but if we deal with our problematic situations ourselves, we can function without leadership from above.

In shared leadership the tasks traditionally belonging to the supervisor can be shared partly or completely by the employees. Shared leadership does not automatically mean that a supervisor should be removed. In some organizations the task of the operative leader has been shared between two people. However, shared leadership mainly means that the tasks of leadership are distributed to more than just one person. Each organization can look at different models and try out which one would suit them best.

When learning shared leadership, curiosity and permitting failure are especially needed. We do not look for a culprit but rather for a solution – we want to help and succeed. When our tools for leadership are current for the 2020's, we can manage change agilely without larger problems. The only considerable problem is our own resistance to change, as with shared leadership we live in constant change. The biggest factor is our own resistance, and we can let go even of that. Another major obstacle is not reacting in time to unpleasant situations, thus making mountains out of molehills.

2

INTRODUCTION

Each organization, company and team need to have functional communication and shared practices. If these are not in order, leadership cannot be shared. The responsibility for rules, guidance and communication cannot be left on the shoulders of one person, the leader.

Shared leadership means working together. Cooperation cannot work without discussion and everyone knowing how things are done.

People often form networks within organizations, and these contacts are primarily used even if the organizational chart would indicate otherwise. Work is then done in one's own circle with familiar colleagues. The purpose of this book is to create understanding about how the organization's leadership model and culture can be molded more into the desired model of operation.

Five Different Ways to Lead

Mankind's leadership has historically evolved alongside the development of technology and culture. Different types of leadership have often been illustrated by separating leadership into five different styles. These styles are presented in the picture below. The blue color in the table shows those sections of the organization managed by a supervisor, and the orange color shows those run by the whole work community.

In leader-centered leadership culture the leader is a very strong individual. Based on mental and physical strength they decide about everything. Organization-centered leadership is based on a hierarchic pattern, of which the army is a good example. This is when the rules are so strong that the personnel can at most affect the division of work itself, while everything else is assigned from above. In these two leadership patterns shouting and even physical contact as a deterrent or encouragement is a commonly accepted way to lead.

Most of the world's organizations reside in a mindset of achievement-centered leadership. On this level the supervisor has understood that they don't have to decide how their subordinates perform their tasks, they just have to set the goals and make the decisions. Dividing up the work, choosing specific tasks and coming up with methods for accomplishing them are all left up to the work community as a whole. The more diligently one works, the faster one can climb up the hierarchy or into other positions with more responsibility and power. The organization acts like a machine: each part of the machine can be swapped out or replaced – nobody is indispensable. An

Leader-centered	Organization-centered	Achievement-centered	Individual-centered	Community-centered
Top-down leadership	Leadership based on a hierarchical chart	Work is guided by competition and achievements	The culture of leadership is family-like and empowering	The culture of leadership is autonomous and functions like a living organism
E.g. the mafia or street gangs	E.g. the army	E.g. innovation work	E.g. tribal culture	E.g. a self-directing organization
Impulsiveness and a strong individual	Strong rules	Goal-oriented management	Coaching management	Community-led methods
Division of work	Division of work	Division of work	Division of work	Division of work
Choosing tasks	Choosing tasks	Choosing tasks	Choosing tasks	Choosing tasks
Methods	Methods	Methods	Methods	Methods
Decisions	Decisions	Decisions	Decisions	Decisions
Values	Values	Values	Values	Values
Goals	Goals	Goals	Goals	Goals
Directing operations	Directing operations	Directing operations	Directing operations	Directing operations

Five different cultures of leadership

organization can also be led based on multiple values, in which case it is an individual-centered culture of leadership. The term "coaching management" describes this level well, where the role of the supervisor has changed into an attending and coaching one. The supervisor is not supposed to make decisions: the employees can make important decisions themselves. The supervisor's task is only to create the right circumstances, enable flexible modes of work, and help employees do their work and to develop their know-how. The values of the organization are built together with the personnel instead of being solely defined by the management.

As we move onto the fifth level, the autonomous community-centered level, the supervisor's role diminishes considerably, and in some cases vanishes altogether. In some community-led organizations there are still titles such as director, but the real leadership is shared so that the titles no longer have any effect on leadership in practice. These new organizations aim at removing fixed responsibilities, but due to legislation and regulations some responsibilities still need to be personified.

On the completely community-led level, after the purpose and aim of the organization have been defined together, the community sets its own goals. The personnel including the executive team are all committed to the work, and everyone has a chance to influence even the purpose and strategies of the organization.

However, the community-led model does not mean that anyone can on the spur of the moment by themselves make significant changes or decide on new guidelines.

Each Way of Leading Is Needed in Some Situations, and There Are Often Several Different Cultures of Leadership Within Organizations

Each level of leadership is equally good, and none of them are better than the others – there are simply different styles of leadership. Each type of leadership is needed in some situations, and often several different cultures of leadership can be found within an organization. We also cannot know how an equivalent chart would look like in a thousand years. It may be possible that the community-centered level may then be considered just as primitive as we now consider the organization-centered model of leadership.

When we talk about shared leadership or bringing the community-led way into organizations, the intent is not to move directly onto the level of com-munity-centered leadership. Shared leadership and community-led methods often mean that we recognize what kind of leadership there is within the organization and what kind of leadership the organization requires conside-ring its purpose and personnel. In this case the model of leadership usually moves towards the right in the above chart. A direct shift into a communi-ty-centered model is an unrealistic goal. Most likely such an attempt would fail much in the same way as a direct shift from the traditional leader-centered model to teamwork would.

There are many cases where the personnel of the organization aren't ready for a new way of working, but long for a more traditional form of leadership. On the other hand, an increasing awareness about different leadership styles will in the long run be reflected in the attitudes of the personnel. Then interest in community-led leadership increases, even if there initially was a desire for more traditional and directive leadership.

Leadership is in a constant state of change, because the individuals who make up the organization are constantly developing. This book will explain how to dismantle the concept of leadership personified in just one person and what is needed in practice to begin sharing leadership.

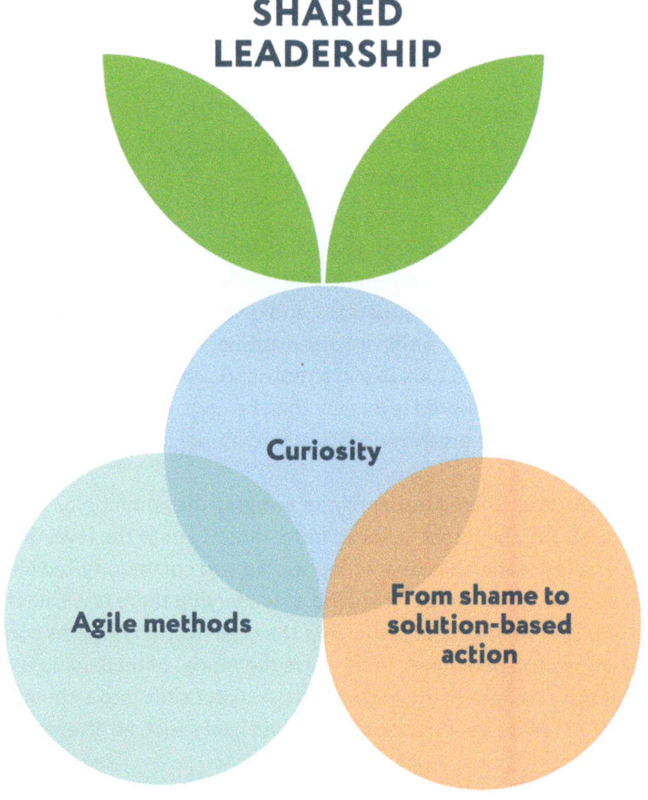

This Book Is Divided Into Four Sections

This book is divided into four sections. Each one complements the previous one, and together they form the cornerstones for shared leadership.

he first chapter describes agility. Agility means taking values, methods, and modern tools into use. The second chapter discusses blaming and shame. The aim of the chapter is to understand the meaning of empathy in the organizational culture and how it affects all the models of operation. With a solution-based approach we can eliminate many problems from the work community, problems which relate to leadership, interaction, interpersonal relations, and doing work.

The third chapter discusses curiosity, and how it functions as a building material in cooperation between people. This chapter talks about innovation, the importance of trying new things and working in pairs as well as the importance of in-house training.

The last chapter presents shared leadership from a practical perspective. Different responsibilities and roles in the organizations are described, along with examples of how the traditional responsibilities and roles can be divided up according to perspective of shared leadership. The chapter also covers different kinds of decision-making models and processes.

This book can be read a bit from here and a bit from there, but to get the best insight it is advised to read it from start to finish in order.

3

AGILE LEADERSHIP

3.1 The Meaning of Agility

Humanness means soft values, empathy, accepting feelings, and appreciati-
on. People today have developed far, and they already have good methods
and tools in use. Creativity, empathy, and feelings without recording and
reproducing the tools and methods to harness them can easily cause
frustration and wasted effort.

This chapter is quite technical, and the beginning may seem dull. You may
move onto the next one and come back later, if this chapter does not seem
interesting now. This chapter will cover what agility means and how it differs
from a traditional leadership model. Some of the most essential concepts are
practices agreed-upon together and the tools offered
by information technology.

Agile methods create shared rules for operations. Without agile methods
these rules would be dictated from above, or each new situation would
require requesting a model of operations from the supervisor. If there is no
supervisor, then each new situation would require gathering the team for a
meeting, which would lead to a constant spiral of meetings – and this is what
shared leadership aims to get rid of.

Variable problems such as e.g. human error or illness cannot be prevented,
but when operations are made agile or flexible, it is possible to react
to changes quicker than before.

Task management means that all essential data regarding the tasks are colle-
cted in one place. There each member of the team
or work group can access it.

3.2 History

Agile project methods were developed around the turn of the millennium.
The main message in the declaration of agility is that it is possible to bring
sensible methods into a stiff and slow-moving traditional organization. At
the same time, the cornerstones of shared leadership have been pondered:
communication and shared practices.

Traditional project models are slow, aiming at planning out everything well
in advanced. However, in the changing world it is impossible to predict
everything beforehand. If a product, project or target is decided on right now

be developed over a year's time, the result may be an outdated tool. Agile project models make sure that the customer gets what they want, and the provider may do and develop its work freely.

The agile manifesto originates from software development. In 2001 17 professionals of the field drafted the manifesto of agile software development (the Agile Manifesto). Based on their experiences they felt they had found better ways to manage their work, when individuals and interaction were valued higher than methods and tools. Likewise software development succeeded better when functional software was valued higher than comprehensive documentation, and customer collaboration was valued higher than contract negotiations. Work also succeeded better when responding to changes was valued over sticking to the plan. Methods, tools, comprehensive documentation and such were of course important, but e.g. interaction and customer collaboration had a greater impact. The models of shared leadership stem from this agile manifesto.

Agility does not mean that documentation and planning are neglected. They are still performed, but flexibly alongside the work itself. At the beginning of a job limits are agreed upon within which the work is allowed to take shape.

It is good to draft a task list in advance, where the tasks first on the list are those to be done first. Therefore, the tasks on top of the list should be gone through more carefully, so that they can be taken on. When new tasks are noted while working, they are added to the list. If they are placed at the end of the list, there is no need to start planning them yet. The task list is constantly updated, so the tasks may change, or new ones may be added as others are completed.

"Work Doesn't Run Out From Doing It"

The agile methods proved to be useful in software development time after time, so they were soon introduced to other fields of industry as well.

Read the manifesto at
agilemanifesto.org

In many sectors it is understood that long text documents which are not changed later aren't that often useful, but what is needed are schematics, drawings and living plans. Plans need to be updated alongside the work. On the other hand, fixed interim goals are also needed.

Fixed interim goals are useful e.g. for limiting the workload. The old saying "work doesn't run out from doing" accurately describes how important it is to learn to limit the workload so that it is suitable for each situation.

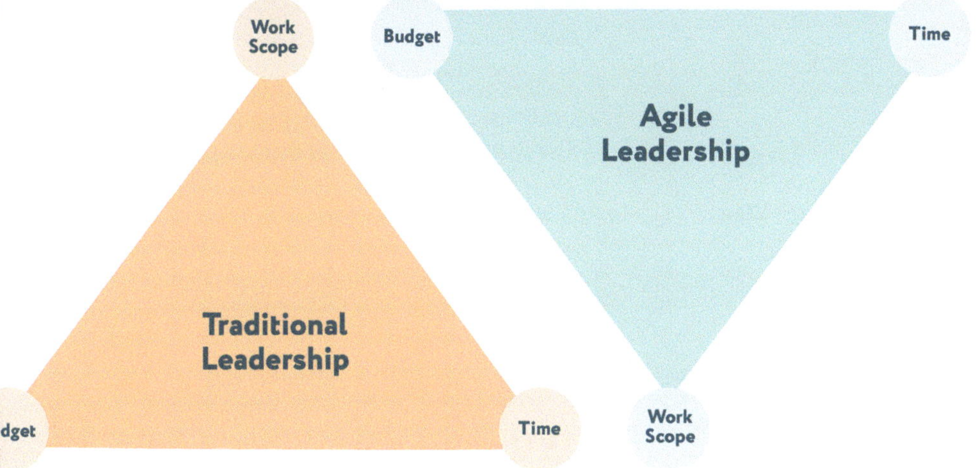

The difference between an agile and a fixed (traditional) project

The chart above shows how work always comprises three factors: the scope of the work, the budget, and the use of time. If they are all fixed, the work itself is fixed. This type of work does not tolerate any surprises or changes.

In an agile project one or more of these factors is flexible. Fixed factors may be e.g. the time or the budget allotted for the project. In reality projects are in fact often prolonged or they exceed their budget – whether it is about construction or IT development. If we lock down only the budget and the time but not the scope of the work, we can determine the latter factor ourselves later.

Many people might think that this is not suitable for e.g. the construction of a house. After all, nobody wants a partly constructed house. In reality the agility of a construction project means that the most important and most necessary tasks are written down on the task list, such as what needs to be finished in the house in order to comply with laws and regulations. This ensures that the vital tasks get done.

How to choose between an agile and a traditional model

When we clearly know the target and the solution, we can use the traditional model: plan first and then carry out the plan; surprises may extend the time needed to carry out the plan or may add to the costs, so a margin of safety is calculated, and the price is determined based on that. This is the normal way when the task has been done many times before and there are few uncertainty factors i.e. variables.

If we know the target well but are not sure about the solution, it is better to choose the agile method. Then we can be certain that we can reach the goal, and we are doing things the right way. While working there will be surprises, but the chosen method guides the work, because it is built for an uncertain environment.

Based on recent years it is easy to see that the world is constantly changing, and often changing faster than ever.

3.3 Methods

The methods of agile leadership include sequencing the work into phases as well as transparency, short efficient meetings, and a common platform to share information. With these anyone joining the work gets up-to-date information, the opportunity to communicate, and directives on how to report or check the situation.

Sometimes even an agile project is worthwhile to be carried out in one long process, but usually the work is better to sequence into phases. Then the interim goals and their deadlines are decided on beforehand. This way the project can be regularly monitored.

Transparency means that everyone taking part in the project can in real time see how the tasks are progressing. Transparency helps all parties of the work understand how the work is progressing. One concrete example of transparency is e.g. the tracking of deliveries. When the client can see that the delivery has not yet been sent and can track where it is, they aren't unnecessarily frustrated and won't e.g. needlessly burden customer service by inquiring after their delivery.

An example of transparency:

Mike and Molly are doing task 1, and they notice that they need to do tasks 2 and 3 before task 1 can be finished. If task 2 is already on the task list, Mike marks it for himself. Task 3 was not found on the task list, so Molly adds it onto the list and marks that she is doing it now.

When anyone from the team looks at the task list, they see that Mike and Molly have started with task 1. They also see that Mike and Molly are also working on tasks 2 and 3.

Maybe it was originally thought that task 1 was to be ready today. However, at the following morning's meeting it turns out that Mike and Molly have not yet been able to complete task 1 because they had to deal with tasks 2 and 3 first. It is then clear to everyone that task 1 is not progressing, task 2 is underway, and the surprise task 3 is also being worked on.

In this way all tasks have been made transparent for the whole team.

Meetings are kept short and efficient, and each meeting focuses on different topics. It is not reasonable to organize long meetings where many different topics are handled. All participants do not have to take part in nearly every meeting, and people get tired in long meetings.

Usually, sequencing the work is used in projects that have a clear beginning and end. It is usually not used in continuous service projects without a clear timeline. Thus, it is worth sequencing a project if it is e.g. a construction project, the development of a mobile application, or the one-time production of a clearly-defined product or service. Non-sequenced work are e.g. customer service or repair services.

A sequenced work project can have cycles of e.g. 1-4 weeks each. In the beginning of a cycle the planning takes place and at the end there is a review. For the initial planning other people than just those working on that cycle are also included. At the end of a cycle interest groups and the people paying for the work are invited to the reviews, to see that the work is progressing. These meetings should be agreed on well in advance and marked in the calendar; in a constantly changing world projects may be prolonged uncontrollably if regularity is not upheld.

It is good to use task lists, file sharing, and instant messaging as shared platforms for information. The rules for how each tool is to be used are agreed on. The criteria for the tasks are defined, such as when the task will be ready and what needs to be done beyond the actual task itself, i.e. is documentation needed, and do any external people or interest groups need to be informed.

3.4 Tools

In agile leadership the best tool is chosen and its use is learned, instead of using the most familiar and easiest tool.

No, no, and for the Last Time No.
Text-based discussion (chat) cannot replace the communication of a team, even though chat may in many situations ease the case considerably. Each team, group, or organization needs to have instant messaging and channels in which to swap ideas quickly on various subjects or jobs. However, chat-type channels cannot be official channels for information, but rather they just replace the corridor talks, where only those speaking are present and others are not.

All work must have an assigned **clear official information channel,** where
all the essential information is organized and structured, and available for
everyone. These information channels must have a person responsible for
them or clear rules for when to use the official channel. Suitable tools for
discussion are e.g. **Microsoft Teams** or **Slack**. In those each topic can be held
in its own thread and connected straight to the work, making it easier to find
necessary info without going to through different chats or e-mail threads.
For example, cats are discussed under the topic of cats, without any
comments on dogs or horses.

In agile work methods no meeting memos are written, unless the law or
regulations specifically demand it. Instead of memos, the task lists are inspected and worked on during meetings. Matters decided on are written directly
to where they will be looked up later. If separate documentation is required,
it will be linked to the task in question, so that it is also found when
that task is being worked on.

E-mail is a tool of the 1990's. It is used when absolutely necessary. It can
be used to send messages between different organizations, when no other
channels are available. Files should be transferred with tools intended for
them and discussions should be held in text-based channels or meetings.
Using e-mail should be avoided whenever there is a faster,
better, and more agile way.

Sending documents i.e. files via e-mail does work when the files do not
change. If the files are edited after being sent or they are worked on together, one should choose **a tool intended for document management**, like
Microsoft Teams, Google Drive, or another application meant for joint work.
These documents can be referred to in internal notifications or instant messaging discussions, but they are never to be shared as such as attachments
to other platforms. If the files or directives are mentioned on physical notice
boards, it would be good to mention where the
document in question is available.

A reference such as "ask person NNN" is bad; the information should be
available at once when needed, and it should not be dependent on another
person's availability. For this reason, all information from the other tools
should be noted down on the task list. If there is discussion about the task
in another tool, a description of it should be transferred onto the task list
immediately and to the right place – especially additional information
and decisions made.

3.5 Task Management

Am I Buying a Pig in a Poke?

Electronic task lists are filled in regardless of time and place. When someone starts on a task, they need to be able to mark the task as started. Comments during work and the end result are noted straight onto the list. If someone wants to know about the status of the task, they do not need to ask the person doing the task directly nor inquire via a chat channel in what state the work is, as it is already visible on the task list.

When all the tasks are added and the information on them is maintained on the task list in real time, we have continuous information about the status of the work. How many tasks are completed, how many are in process, and how many are not yet done? If new tasks appear, they are noted onto the list and the workload grows. This is what transparency means.

Often the task lists are also opened for the interest groups or clients. If the customer has bought "a pig in a poke", meaning that they have fixed the budget and the allotted time but not the extent of the work, they need to know what they are getting for their money.

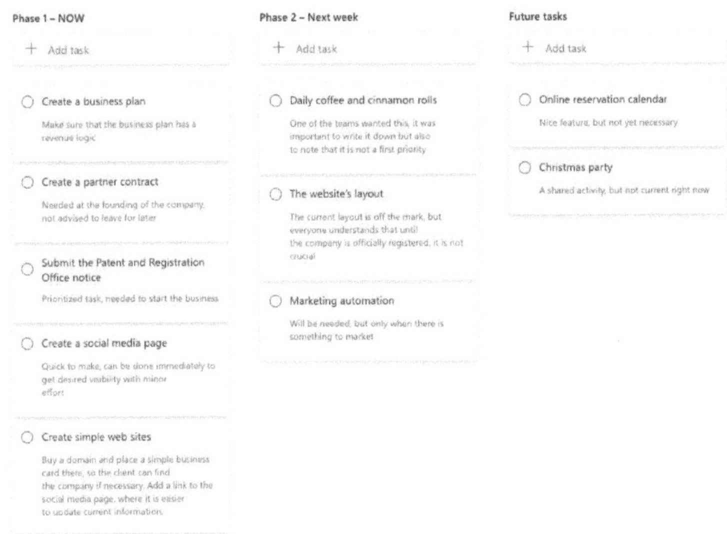

An example of the task list of a start-up company after the first meeting (the Microsoft Planner tab in Teams)

The previous image presents the tasks of a new company after the first meeting. In this case it was decided to create three silos for the tasks: what needs to be done right now, what will be done next week, and what will be done some time in the future. People discuss and agree on what will be done, someone writes the tasks down and places them onto the task list.

When the tasks are discussed, extra information is added to them and they are placed into order of importance. Here the most important tasks are on the left side. Finally it is decided who does what, and when the next meeting will take place. All tasks are not necessarily assigned to anyone, so anyone may take a task for themselves when they have the time for it. Everyone's tasks are noted, but because e.g. a Christmas party is not a current event, it will be handled later.

Calendar or Task List?

A calendar is an important tool, but it cannot replace the task list. One can allocate time into the calendar for when to work on the project or another larger unit, if the employee can't work on the project full-time. With the calendar it is also possible to decide on meetings among several people so that they can sequence their day and tasks. It is not worth putting fixed tasks onto the calendar, as task lists exist for that.

When one takes the next available task for oneself from the task list, it is not yet possible to know how the rest of the task list will turn out. Especially if the work is done by several people at the same time, the order of the tasks may change. Different tasks are also done simultaneously. It is important to look at the task list every time a task is completed or started. This is to avoid having two people doing the same task.

Task lists can be made for almost any kind of work, whether fixed or agile. It is easy to update a task list, and it is easy to share to others.

Different tools are needed for different kinds of work. Using the tools must be trained, and if necessary the tools should be changed for better ones. The same rules apply to task lists. Nobody can use them effectively without training. Be merciful with yourselves and others. Give guidance and explain how to do better, don't embarrass or point out errors.

An example of the task list to build a playhouse

The above picture presents the task list for building a playhouse. The project resembles a fixed project more than an agile one, as we know the target and the method. The order of the tasks may be changed though, and new tasks can be brought in to fill the gaps. The meetings are ideally held at the beginning of each phase, i.e. before planning, preparations, implementation, and maintenance.

Good task list tools are taken into use quickly, bad ones are dropped just as quickly. However, everyone needs to commit to trying out new methods. It may be hard to get a volunteer construction group to use the task list. Then the list functions as a personal tool for the project leader. But when in paid employment, more commitment to the tools can be demanded of the employees.

The biggest resistance is usually in the person's mind. Being in a hurry cannot be an obstacle for taking a new tool into use – often it is just an excuse for laziness. If being in a hurry is a real reason, other tasks are to be postponed in order to get the right tools into use.

The task list needs to be visible for everyone during meetings so that they can learn by example how to use it and what its true effect is which benefits everyone.

3.6 Short Status Meetings and Fixed Meetings

A few fixed meetings as well as meetings held as necessary are required to
decide on matters. When the pace of work is hectic and matters proceed
quickly, it is good to start the day with a short status meeting. During these
you go through what was done yesterday, what everyone is doing today, and
whether there are any problems or obstacles for doing it. The tasks on the
task lists should mainly be ones that take less than a whole day's work. If
somebody is doing the same task for two days, it should raise the question
whether something is wrong and why they haven't been able to
move on to the following task.

On the other hand, we have several projects and some proceed slower. In
that case, the status meetings can be held twice or three times a week, but
with the same idea. At the status meetings the aim is not to handle details,
but to keep the meetings at less than 15 minutes. After this it is possible for
those more involved in the problems to discuss them. The rest of the team
do not need to spend more time on that discussion.

In the beginning of work phases it would be important to get everyone involved to go through and plan their work. The aim is to ponder all possible tasks
that are connected to the next phase. Sometimes something extra that had
to be done as well might not be noticed until during the work process itself.
The aim is to get as many of these hidden tasks onto the task list as possible
already beforehand. This helps in finding out whether it is even theoretically
possible to have the planned work done within the following work phase.

Practices of the Short Meetings

If the supervisor just announces the rules and practices, the others have a
hard time just taking them in and remembering them afterwards. The practices of a team or work group should be gone through once for half an hour,
the rules for the short meetings should be discussed. People commit easier
to rules agreed on together than to ones just given from above.

It is recommended not to use mobile phones or smart devices at meetings,
and to keep webcams on during online meetings. Even these rules are not
as effective when simply handed out as when they are agreed on together.
Absences from meetings are often due to bad leadership, inefficiency of the
meetings, or meetings held unnecessarily.

  ✗ *Talk about everything just in case.*

  ✗ *Invite everyone just in case.*

  ✗ *This might have something to do with us / interest the listeners.*

  ✗ *I'll just come up with a topic for the meeting on the fly, since I have no time to prepare.*

Favor these

  ✔ *Postpone the meeting if you do not have time to prepare it.*

  ✔ *Postpone the meeting if you do not know what to talk about in it.*

  ✔ *Postpone the meeting if you are unsure of whom to invite to it.*

  ✔ *Invite the people that you really need.*

  ✔ *Ask those who may be needed. Give them a chance to decide for themselves whether to attend or to do something else instead. When the right people are present and the correct issues are handled, there is a high motivation to participate and a high commitment to the tasks.*

All meetings are recommended to have a rotating duty to lead them. The supervisor may have to be flexible, but the rotating duty is beneficial. That way everybody learns the challenges of leading a meeting. When everyone knows when their turn to lead is coming, they prepare and focus on the meeting in a completely different way. When you have led a meeting, you know what it feels like when someone talks beside the topic or rambles on. Beginning the habit of rotating the duty may feel laborious, but it will reward you after a few rounds.

It is everybody's responsibility to have effective and sensible meetings. Be merciful to each other and practice. When a work group finds its own conventions, leading the meetings starts to run smoothly. New members have an easy time integrating, as anyone in the group can advise how to act at our meetings. Maybe an eager person has written down the conventions and can give them to the newcomer.

One should not be afraid of organizing a meeting if there is a clear need for it. If some matter is talked over for too long, e.g. in chat, it is easier to organize e.g. an online meeting and handle the matter properly together and decide on it. For instance, when organizing holiday accommodation among a group of friends, it is more sensible to collect the options and have a 15-minute meeting where the options are discussed and then decide the resort rather than writing opinions on WhatsApp for a week and try to deduce from there what the majority's opinion is and who will make the decision.

3.7 Towards Soft Values

Nowadays people talk about information overload. There is too much information, and it is pouring in from everywhere. If the flood of new information at work is too great, it may cause frustration and even anxiety when one is not able to focus on one's own work. Time is spent on digesting and organizing that information.

The right knowledge to the right people and the rest for the ones seeking it is a good and important principle along which communication should be implemented.

In the face of an information overload people start to automatically reject unnecessary information. At its worst people shut down all listening and all digesting of knowledge to protect their mind from that overload. Problems occur when people are no longer available, they do not answer messages, nor take any part in discussions. This is why shared rules are needed for what information is shared and through which channels.

A memory list for agile leadership

- *Favor short meetings*
- *Choose the meeting participants carefully*
- *No e-mail, use better and agreed-on tools for communication*
- *When dealing with complicated matters call, or organize a meeting*

A memory list for agile task management

- *All tasks in one place*
- *Everyone has easy access to the task list*
- *Everyone gets to edit and create new tasks on the list*
- *All information relating to the tasks is added directly to the list*
- *All new information is put on the task list immediately*
- *Everyone notes on the list when starting a task*
- *Everyone notes on the list when they finish a task*

To be able to follow the rules, we need to have understanding towards each other. Mere rules sond routines are just half of the work between people. The next chapter handles why it is often so difficult to obey the rules and what is needed in addition to the routines.

4

BLAMING AND SHAME

4.1 A National Disease

In many work communities there are people behaving badly, who create a negative atmosphere. They often get trust and attention from others, as they – sometimes rightfully – criticize the work and the leadership.

Their means for that is pointing the blame at others, which often activates a feeling of guilt in people. In Finland the upbringing used and still uses guilt as a method, and it could even be called a national disease. Many are accustomed to this, and do not know how to limit blaming in their work life. Problems are created for the whole work community if the supervisor leads by pointing the blame at their employees.

There is a cure to eradicating the blaming as it causes feelings of shame and passivity. Let everyone influence the work and leadership. Then the power of these proverbial birds of ill omen is diminished, there is no room for them to spoil the motivation nor the atmosphere. When everyone can influence the problems and defects, the complainer has to look in the mirror instead of blaming others.

When colleagues are feeling better it shows outwards, and the positive atmosphere increases. One must understand, though, that the change takes a long time. These kinds of attitudes and problems related to interpersonal relationships are not solved in a flash.

4.2 Failure

Why Are People Afraid of Failure?

If a failure is followed by negative feedback, one starts to avoid failure.

When the feedback is formulated wrong, it sounds like the failing person is bad as a person. Shame and rejection are among our greatest fears, as we are coded in our DNA to be herd animals. Being rejected or abandoned by one's own herd is the worst. Such a feeling can even be felt physically in the body.

In recent years, transparency has increased, as a new kind of open and more permissive culture has been created in organizations, where instead of loo- king for guilty ones, solutions are looked for together. Additionally personnel are trained in giving and receiving constructive feedback and in treating others in a more dignified way. However, the hardest thing is to handle self-criticism, as you cannot escape it. When one's own mind is lashing oneself, one often tries to avoid failure and won't even try to solve problems.

Lack of Internal Empathy

Self-discipline and self-criticism are often confused, or they are thought to be the same thing. The table below presents how self-discipline and self-criticism are two different things.

The purpose of self-discipline is to direct a person towards a goal. One will stick to the limits set by oneself. Too much self-criticism, on the other hand, claims that one is a bad person.

Many people think that self-criticism is a means to motivate oneself. A better method for internal motivation would be the opposite of self-criticism, i.e. internal empathy. One has be able to be merciful to oneself in failures. Mistakes happen to those who do things.

Self-discipline or self-criticism?

Self-criticism is the inadequate ability to be consciously present in one's body and to appease oneself with healthy habits.

Self-discipline takes you towards the goal and allows for flexibility if necessary	Self-criticism is the opposite of internal empathy, not of self-discipline
In self-discipline one sets goals for oneself	Self-criticism tells you why you did not succeed
With self-discipline one avoids quick reliefs	Self-criticism blames you for wanting a quick relief
With self-discipline one maintains the boundaries set for oneself	Self-criticism is modelled on our educators' critical nature, not a tool for maintaining boundaries

The table shows the differences between self-discipline and self-criticism

When we learn to be compassionate towards ourselves, we learn to be compassionate towards others. On the emotional level we should have this model trained for when we or someone else makes a mistake at work. If our first feeling after a mistake is negative, we probably convey that feeling onwards. We cannot hide our feelings; they are unconsciously expressed by our demeanor and our communication.

By increasing our internal compassion we can encourage ourselves and others in the event of a mistake. We can understand and accept that mistakes sometimes happen when the aim is development and reaching the goal. When mistakes cause a feeling of compassion, we dare to make mistakes again instead of being afraid of them. Then we try harder, we boldly dare to take risks, and we reach higher. Sometimes we even exceed ourselves and reach great achievements.

Increasing internal compassion i.e. empathy is a slow process and requires practice. The first step is to understand what it is about and to observe one's own inner voice. The goal of this book is not to guide to empathy, but to enlighten about its meaning behind failure. Without empathy the circle of shame – blaming oneself and others – will continue. Without empathy we also allow others to uphold a negative culture.

4.3 A Solution-Based Approach

By understanding the background of the fear of failure we understand why it is still common in organizations to look for culprits rather than looking for solutions. Nobody wants to be a failure or be rejected. People often feel it is more important to ensure one's place in the herd through one's actions rather than to look for a solution to a problem. In shared leadership we do not point the blame, but we are rather looking for solutions to solve the problems.

Am I Replaceable?

In the achievement-centered leadership which was presented in the beginning of this book the replaceability of people affects operations. According to the thought pattern behind the model everyone is replaceable. People are parts in a machine, which can be replaced when a part does not work i.e. when a person makes enough mistakes. In such an atmosphere people are competing and trying to point the blame at others. Putting oneself up and blaming others creates an impression that one is performing better in work life than others. When one shows one's necessity to the supervisor, one's own work may get easier.

This thought pattern sounds brutal as the general awareness of pluralistic leadership has increased. People need to understand that pointing the blame at others is not a solution. It is more important to ponder a solution to a problem and afterwards work out how to avoid the situation in the future. It does not matter who caused the problem. It is more important to make sure that the problem does not repeat itself. The person in question does of course get feedback. When the feedback is given in the right way, in the right place, and in a constructive fashion, the person can take it as a learning experience instead of guilt.

Even in this issue we need to be merciful towards ourselves. The thought pattern behind goal-oriented leadership has been learned from previous generations, and in many situations the pattern of goal-oriented leadership takes place. Even if we understand the importance of pluralistic leadership in theory, making it a reality is challenging if the old patterns from within occur in everything else.

Culture of Innocence

To dismantle the blaming of others an internal change or a change in the sur-rounding culture is needed. When a person is going through these matters within themselves, they can cope with a guilt-seeking environment without feeling the blame on themselves. On the other hand, we cannot force anyone to grow as a human being. We can however make sure that values of internal compassion and a culture of innocence are brought forward in the work environment.

Getting rid of blaming others needs to be trained in work communities and teams. When someone expresses a blaming comment, one needs to be careful not to condemn or blame that person. The matter can be brought up one-on-one in order to give the person a chance to realize what went wrong. We cannot silence everyone, but we can teach people to recognize their own behavior and correct their actions. Each member of the work community is responsible for the atmosphere, which means that each person can gently remind the group that we are not looking for the culprit but for the solution.

4.4 Problems with Delivering

The core reason for problems with delivering is almost always some original, unconscious problem, the solving which would avoid other problems. Other difficulties are often only consequences of the original problem.

If matters are not looked into enough, repairing the follow-up problems
does not help, as the core reason produces new problems all the time. The
problems with delivering need to be thoroughly inspected and it needs to be
asked as many times as necessary why they appear
and from where they come.

Being in a hurry and having too tight schedules have many causes. Sick
leave and changing situations create additional challenges, but usually the
underlying causes are too large performance goals and unrealistic schedules.
When there is no flexibility in the schedules or work is done with too small a
margin, even a small problem may cause exceptions
to the workload estimates.

When one just clocks into work and is not responsible for the results,
solving problems is the responsibility of others. It goes without saying that
the work leader at a construction site may quickly assess the work, as he
understands the big picture and has the best experience of that situation.
If the workers are asked, it takes them some time to ponder the answer,
because they know that they are not responsible for it. The answer may be
too limited in order to give a good impression. The answer may be too vast in
order to cover their own backs out of fear of failure.

A solution to problems with delivering
1. *Measure the speed of the work and renew the workload assessment*

2. *Teach the workers to measure and assess the workload*

3. *Transfer the responsibility for measuring and assessing the workload for
   those doing the work*

In shared leadership people get to influence their own work and they understand the premises for creating schedules. If the person doing the work
in question is included in making and assessing the workload, they are better
committed to the timetables. Everyone wants to follow schedules and plans
that they themselves have made. It is harder to take on a predefined schedu-
le – especially if it feels impossible to follow it.

How to commit people to solve problems?
1. *Bring up the problems at a meeting – do not complain while working. If
   dealing with the problem does not suit the meeting, ask when the matter can
   be dealt with, or ask for a separate meeting to handle the problem*

2. *Let people ponder together for solutions to the problems*

3. Lead others towards what you need – do not immediately give your own solutions or proposals

4. Participate in the discussion as just one of the others, and share your own opinions

5. Agree together on common practices for how to solve or report the problem in the future

6. If the problems still arise, repeat this model and propose your own solution for it more clearly

Problems mentioned by employees may seem insignificant from the point of view of others. One needs to understand that a problem brought up by anyone is a problem in the delivery chain. If these problems are not solved, that may cripple the quality of the whole delivery.

There are several different techniques for finding out the root causes – some easier and some harder. It is surely possible to find the right method for each field. If a method is too hard to start on, a lighter method of problem solving can be used. A common way is to organize regular, reflective meetings where the work done is inspected and everyone's comments are taken into consideration.

4.5 Reflective Meetings

A reflective meeting is a regular meeting where the delivery team gathers and ponders the actual doing of the work. In phased projects these are to be held after each phase. For fixed teams it is recommended to organize reflective meetings at least four times a year.

Reflective meetings offer an opportunity to deal with any mistakes. Constantly pointing out the mistakes while working only worsens the speed of delivery.

It is worth reserving time for the reflective meetings and having some warm-up tasks to start with. People need to feel secure and open, and free to speak their minds at the meeting.

If possible, arrange the reflective meeting somewhere else than the working environment. Reserve a cabinet room from a restaurant or some other space that is physically detached from the workplace. If held as an online meeting, reflective meetings should not be combined with other meetings.

If the reflective meetings are organized after each phase, one hour is enough for its duration. If the reflective meetings are organized less than once a month, it is advised to reserve two hours.

It is good to reserve 10-15 % of the meeting's duration for the warm-up tasks. The idea of the warm-up task is to give everyone a chance to say something and share something about themselves or their mindset at that moment. Some examples:

- *What animal would reflect you right now?*
- *If you were a logo of a company, what would you be right now?*
- *Where would you travel for vacation?*
- *What would you do if you won the lottery and got 10,000 €?*
- *What new hobby would you want to take up?*
- *What color would you choose to describe your current feeling?*

There are three themes to go through at reflective meetings. The first theme concerns past successes, the quality of which you want to uphold or develop. The second theme concerns matters requiring development or which gone wrong somehow. The third theme concerns new models of action that are to be tried out during the following phase.

Each participant should produce thoughts and ideas at the meeting. One participant guides the others, and the others produce. At online meetings a tool called Miro is used, and at face-to-face meetings Post-It –notes on the wall can be used. For instance, the participants are given 15 minutes to fill in notes on different topics. After this everyone gets a turn to talk about their notes. The notes can be discussed in either a person-by-person or a per-topic order.

Regarding the matters requiring development, it is good to ponder the reasons for why the problems have arisen and how they can be avoided in the future. A light root-cause analysis is done while people's negative feelings regarding what happened are gone through.

Finally one or two targets for development are chosen for the next phase. All defects cannot be changed, as it would be too hard. But it is important to discuss what the biggest problem is and to focus on preventing that before the next reflective meeting.

At the next reflective meeting there is no need to look at past output or to
copy topics from previous meetings. Each reflective meeting
is an entity of its own.

The author of this book has planned a coaching for training
reflective short meetings and trying out different models.
You can find additional information at
www.karlex.fi/reflektiivinen

4.6 Towards Liberation

Blaming others and the feeling of shame are learned models that guide our
thinking and communication. It is possible to unlearn them, and instead
learn more empathetic ways to handle work-related situations. Guilt usually
arises reactively, from the spine so to speak.

The best way to handle one's own communication is to halt.

Halting means conscious presence. Methods for this are e.g. yoga, medita-
tion, mindfulness, sports, walking, or any other exercise or doing where the
person focuses on sensing what they are feeling. By understanding one's
own emotional state one can more easily choose how to
communicate with others.

If You Have Nothing Good to Say, Say Nothing at All

This old saying about staying silent if you have nothing good to say is usually
still valid. This advice could be adjusted so that while working it's better to
stay silent, as long as the faults don't pose a great risk to anyone. The faults
can be written down and brought up at reflective meetings. If there are no
such meetings, it is advised to ask the supervisor or the team members when
it would be appropriate to go through matters of development.

Everyone is responsible for their own emotions. We cannot protect others
endlessly. We can however choose how to communicate so that we do not
intentionally irritate or offend others with our words. When shame or guilt
are lurking the back of our minds, they may cause us to react primitively in
order to protect ourselves. It is allowed to talk to others about one's feelings.
Many are surprised to hear how much the others are experiencing
the same feelings as they are.

5

CURIOSITY AND COLLABORATION

5.1 The Starting Point for Learning

Curiosity is the Starting Point for Learning

When a mind wants to know something new, it directs its motivation towards that new matter. Curiosity has provided an advantage for surviving compared to a non-curious person. Curious people come up with new solutions and they dare to try out new methods. They are not afraid to fail. Curiosity is a quality that can be increased and strengthened.

The previous chapter explained why people are afraid of failures. When a person learns how to halt and erase one's fears, curiosity awakens and ways of action change accordingly. When the mental locks are removed, new desires, needs, and qualities are revealed from within.

People often have the misconception that by doing this and that concrete matter they can erase the present anxiety and indisposition. Everyone should understand that by improving life quality, well-being is increased, and then concrete matters cannot cause bad feelings in the same way that they used to. Curiosity and the skill to generate ideas arise when a person is feeling well.

Children ask on average about 107 questions an hour. It is no wonder that they learn so quickly and so much. As they age, people lose their curiosity. They no longer dare to ask bold questions, so as not to seem dumb in the eyes of the other. When we learn to detach from shame, we dare to be open to uncertainty and vulnerability. Then learning takes place.

5.2 Innovation

Innovation is systematically repeated curiosity. The aim is to produce new solutions, services, or products.

Innovation can be created purposefully or inadvertently. The most effective way is to create suitable circumstances to help new ideas to well up from the depths of the mind. Innovation can be lightly and agilely started in many ways.

In organizations various research and development departments can be started for the purpose of innovation. At these departments shared leadership and community-led leadership are often utilized, because the operations at these departments may often seem unclear and uncontrollable while innovating. If the organization is otherwise hierarchic, the innovation departments are separated from the normal hierarchy so that they can function fruitfully.

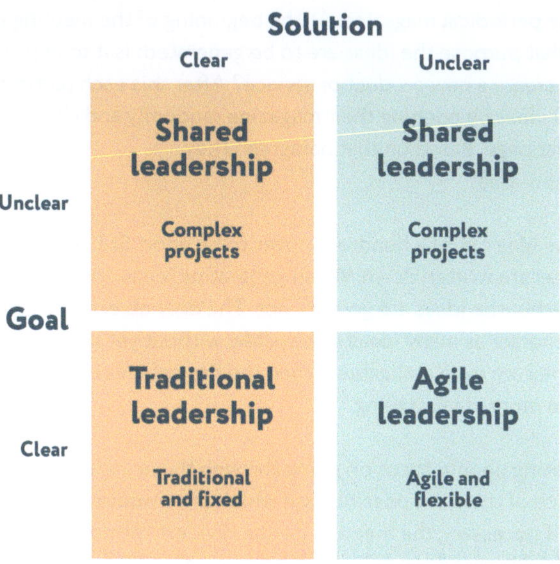

How to choose a model of leadership when the goal is unclear

In complex and unclear projects the extent of the work is not fixed. Only the time, sharing of tasks, and monitoring the work can be controlled. When innovating the agile leadership model can be utilized e.g. in such a way that the work is phased, and daily short meetings as well as planning and review meetings are held.

Innovation Process

Innovation can also be implemented lightly by reserving some two-hour meetings for a select group. The theme of the meetings is to gather ideas and refine them into products. The aim of innovation is to first produce a lot of ideas, after which some of them are chosen for further development. There the ideas are inspected in more detail and their further realization is planned. Finally, one or two ideas are selected to be carried out, and their implementation is planned.

For the first meeting someone needs to familiarize themselves with various means of producing ideas. They will prepare and give advice to the others. One example is an exercise with the help of a magazine. Each participant brings along one periodical magazine. At the beginning of the meeting it is agreed on for what purpose the ideas are to be generated: is it to improve functions, or to create a new product or service? After this each participant generates 10-20 ideas by opening their magazine randomly and choosing a paragraph on that page. Based on that paragraph they
should write a new idea.

Usually only one idea out of a hundred proves to be good. Still, even the most insane ideas are written down. When generating ideas one should not think about whether the ideas are good or not. The only objective of this meeting is to generate as many ideas as possible, without yet taking a stand as to whether they are even realizable. When the flow of ideas starts, there will be more and more ideas coming.

At the next meeting people focus on going through those generated ideas and ponder which of them are possible and which ones would have value in realizing them. If necessary, the meeting can be divided into smaller groups for going over the ideas and choosing the ones to realize. After this the po-tential ideas are looked over together and a handful, less than ten, are select-ed to be worked on further. Important criteria for the selection are whether those ideas fit the nature and values of the organization and whether we have the willingness to carry them out. A quick cost calculation and profit estimation or the effect on the organization's operations are
also part of this process.

At the last meeting these less than ten ideas are first gone through and one or two are selected for further processing. The rest of the meeting is used for further planning those ideas and pondering how to progress the matter in one's own organization.

At the beginning of each meeting, it is recommended to have a warm-up task as suggested in chapter 4.5. Reflective Meetings.

With this method it is ensured that the organization invests in innovation and that good ideas are realized. In some communities there is e.g. no time nor opportunity to innovate due to urgent schedules. In other communities there may be lots of ideas, but nobody takes a catch on them, and throwing ideas around is mostly just a means for invigoration.

I am an active member in an association, where during one autumn I sat at three successive brainstorming meetings. Every time there were great ideas, but not even one was carried forward. We had wasted three evenings as well as two months in the calendar in the middle of our busiest years, but the project for the following year was not chosen. Finally, after a couple of months, the chairperson and me forcibly introduced a new project model by ourselves – even though there had been every opportunity for everyone to agree together on the project and the methods for carrying it out, and everyone could have been mentally committed to them.

In professional innovation it is not just fun and games. Innovation requires not just creativity and freedom but also the methods to generate ideas and to process them further.

5.3 A Culture of Experimentation

A culture of experimentation means an environment that allows and enables trying out all new kinds of methods of operation. Without curiosity no one is eager to try out new things. In a culture of experimentation everyone can suggest a different approach, and the others are supportive of experimentation. The experimentation does not have to be a success, as even a failed experimentation is a learning experience, and one can be grateful for the experiences. The opposite of a culture of experimentation is a culture of planning, where everything is investigated thoroughly before taking action.

Within the organization it is advised to think beforehand about how to handle feelings of shame and failure. If the result in the culture of experimentation is a complete fiasco, it is then known in advance how to treat the people involved and how to motivate them to continue on despite the failure.

Organizations in general should have the knowledge and tools to handle different emotions. In the spirit of a culture of experimentation, I recommend doing a short exercise in a small group.

1. *Print out cards with the names and description of emotions, available for free at* **www.karlex.fi/tunnekortit**

2. *Cut each emotion along with its description into its own paper slip*

3. *Gather the group*

4. *Everyone in turn takes a slip and reads the description, and the others try to guess what emotion it is*

5. *Discuss among the group how this emotion is present at the workplace and how these emotions are usually reacted to*

6. *Each one describes how they want to be treated when they are experiencing this emotion*

7. *Write down the shared opinions of the team about how to deal with various emotions*

An Exercise about Feelings

The culture of experimentation calls for reporting, especially if the experimentation requires resources or funding from the organization. Everyone has the right to experiment but also a duty to present the results of that experimentation to the others. The culture of experimentation is not a free pass for doing fun things at work. The experimentation must always have the goal of improving the wellbeing or the operations of the organization.

In a culture of experimentation it is possible to enact light innovation or start with a completely new idea. The most important thing in the culture of experimentation is to maintain people's enthusiasm and interest. This will work as the glue between the people and commit them to the organization. By enabling different experimentations, the organization is telling the employees that we care about your opinions, and we take suggestions seriously.

Shared Leadership as an Experiment

In hierarchic organizations there is a clear organizational structure and a strong position of a supervisor, as presented earlier in this book regarding leader-, organization- and achievement-oriented organizations. When the shift towards individual-oriented or community-led organization is desired, the change is made carefully through experimentation.

In a hierarchic organization it is possible to build community-led groups i.e. self-guided teams featuring shared leadership.

It is possible within teams to share the supervisor's responsibility among the team members, and when the model has begun to function, new teams without a supervisor can be formed. These teams function side by side with the traditional teams in the organization. Each employee may suggest what kind of or which team they want to be part of. With the help of the culture of experimentation and the forerunner teams it is possible to obtain experience on how shared leadership works in practice in one's organization.

The culture of experimentation questions the basic method of developmental R&D operations, benchmarking. In benchmarking the already-existing is repeated and copied, trusting the old model will work. Conversely in the culture of experimentation things is done without being fully sure of the outcome. We can however currently benchmark one of the most well-known community-led organizations, Buurtzorg. It employs 15,000 people divided into 10-12 person community-led teams. The teams are served by about 50 people at the central organization. The teams may autonomously decide on everything, as long as the customers and the organization benefit from it.

A community-led approach can be tried in the name of the culture of experimentation, and at its best the new method of operations may spread to the whole organization. In some organizations even the board of directors have embraced shared leadership. If business operations and the strategy of the organization are of interest, any employee may seek to join the board of directors and act as a part of it.

5.4 Working in Pairs

When working in pairs one should show interest in the other person's work methods and know-how.

Employees working on similar things often end up as work pairs. However, it would be more essential that the work pairs complement each other's know-how. Working tightly together with someone else is bound to raise some curiosity towards the other person and their skills.

A work pair can be formed to increase the know-how, so that one person mentors and the other person learns new things. Working as a pair can also be based on a topic, interest, or technology. Sometimes working together may be mainly based on friendship. Friendship may often also be curiosity – a beautiful curiosity.

Advice Regarding the Work Pair

The most important thing regarding the work pair is not that they always take your side, but that they dare to give constructive feedback, even in front of others, when you are about to make a mistake. When a deep trust has been formed, even being wrong is seen as just a work issue. Everyone in the team knows that everyone can be wrong occasionally. The most important thing is to find the mistakes quickly and to correct them, not just not making them.

In shared leadership it is recommended to find a work pair. It is not necessary to share everything with everyone, so as to not burden the others too much. When you have a trustee whom you can always quickly spar on matters with, working gets easier. In a good work pair you also take responsibility for the other person's coping: "Take a break and rest a bit."

5.5 Orientation

New employees need to learn to work according to the organization's methods.

Whose Task is Orientation?

Leading is guiding others, giving them advice, and helping them. Orientation is a very important task, where a new person is committed to the company's methods of operation. Way too often orientation is neglected due to busy schedules or done by someone who does not themselves do the work in question. In many organizations the orientation is focused just on general matters. Only later will the colleagues then train the new person alongside doing the actual work.

What if the Employees Handled the Orientation of the Newcomer?

In shared leadership everyone may take part in decision-making and development. Because of this it is common to spontaneously find people willing to give advice. Nobody needs to be explicitly tasked to give advice to new employees, because people have learned that action is taken when needed.

The most curious ones are usually the most active ones, as they want to get to know their new colleagues.

The whole company or the whole team benefits from an inspired person using their work time to train a new employee in the practices of the organization and the work itself. The new person gets an inspired and happy colleague as well as up-to-date advice and best practices.

How to Screen for People interested in Orientation?

People-oriented individuals are social, and conversing with others comes naturally for them. Fact-oriented people enjoy being experts, i.e. a job well done. There are people in both groups who want to guide others to get them started.

1. *Talk openly about the need for orientation – bring the matter up every now and then*

2. *After a suitable time, organize a meeting where you invite people to ponder the aims of orientation and to solve the problems of it*

3. *At the meeting*

    a. *Ask everyone to describe what they didn't understand when they were orientated*

    b. *Ask what everyone would like to add to the orientation*

    c. *Ask if anyone still has any ideas or thoughts about orientation*

4. *Collect the received material, don't try to solve everything, and don't yet recruit any people to the orientation team. The volunteers would have announced themselves by now if interested*

5. *Assess the entirety, i.e. what the orientation should include – and put all the thoughts in writing*

6. *During the following weeks ask about who would be interested in collecting the material received at the meeting (see point 3)*

7. *Arrange a meeting for those interested and give them free reigns to gather the material and even to make a preliminary proposal for new orientation instructions*

5.6 Towards Community-Led orientation

Curiosity is the starting point for many things, and without it developing the operations of an organization would be considerably harder. Curiosity is a sign of good self-esteem and of the courage to do things in one's own way or in a new way. Curiosity is needed for learning and experimentation. Learning and experimentation are needed for producing new information and skills.

The culture of experimentation provides the prerequisites for self-guided learning and the freedom to think outside the box. When people step out of the line and differentiate themselves, miraculous things start to happen. Curious people also dare to lead others.

The first impression is important for a new employee, as it often defines the starting points of their career in the organization.

Curiosity cannot be given space unless it is first understood what prevents it. These obstacles are e.g. blaming and shame (see chapter 4). Curiosity is not a random characteristic, but rather it can be reinforced by looking for solutions and keeping short reflective meetings to get rid of those practices of the organization which inhibit curiosity.

If the leadership and tools of the organization are not up-to-date, soft values on their own are not enough to make community-led orientation work. The organization must have clear methods as well as mutually agreed-upon practices and tools for dismantling the tasks of supervisors in order to increase community-led orientation.

This book has presented the backgrounds, the prerequisites, and the techniques for community-led orientation. The next chapter will present shared leadership, which at its best is community-led and autonomous leadership.

SHARED LEADERSHIP

Curiosity

Agile methods

From shame to solution-focused functions

6.1 A Leap into the Uncontrolled

Shared leadership literally means that the leadership is shared. The operations of the organization are not uncontrolled: matters are agreed on beforehand, power and responsibility are given to those who want it. For many traditional directors the uncontrolled nature of the whole may initially feel a bit scary and distressing, when the threads are no longer in one's own hands. The purpose is to free up time for the director to do other things and to ponder larger matters.

A trip to the summer cabin is natural form of shared leadership – nobody controls the whole or tells the others what to do, when, and with whom.

One of the friends gets the idea to go to a summer cabin. They start to look for a place, and send a message to their friends: "Should we go to a summer cabin?" Discussion takes place, and the time for the trip as well as other participants are pondered. A place and a time are decided together.

If somebody loves food or considers it is important, they will ask how to organize the food situation. They may suggest that the others pay a given sum, and the person in question will do the shopping. Cooking turns are divided among those interested.

A devoted fisherman asks the others about their interest in fishing. They rent a boat, and get the spinning rods and other gear to the location. The costs will be shared among those going fishing.

One person in the group loves the sauna. They start chopping wood the moment they get to the cabin. The sauna gets heated already in the afternoon, even though it was originally discussed to have it in the evening. But they are not blamed, but on the contrary, they get praised for chopping the wood, and some people had already washed themselves before the proper sauna in the evening.

The following table presents a table already featured in this book, but in an extended form. The new table shows that there are some shared areas in different types of leadership. However, when sharing leadership, the meaning and the methods of working in these subsections changes. Comparing e.g. the method of selecting tasks in an organization- and an individual-centered leadership type, there is a large difference; in the individual-centered leadership the tasks are created together and not necessarily as straightforwardly as when it is done by just one person.

In the table below the individual- and community-centered leadership models represent shared leadership. In these cultures of leadership there may be supervisors, but their power is reduced, and it has been shared among the personnel.

	Leader-centered	Organization-centered	Achievement-centered	Individual-centered	Community-centered
Division of work	A strong individual decides who does what	People may decide who does what	Everyone chooses or earns their role	Everyone is asked what they want to do	Everyone does what feels right for themselves
Choosing tasks	The boss hands out the tasks	The supervisor assigns the tasks	People get to choose their own tasks	Tasks are created together	Anyone may create and carry out tasks
Methods	Given from above	Orientation and the rules explain	Are the responsibility of the person doing the work	Pondered together	Are chosen freely, and advice is asked form others if necessary
Decisions	Done by one person	Based on status and role	Are brought to the supervisor, if one does not have a mandate oneself	Made together	Made through an advisory process
Values	Given from above, accepted without questioning	Are derived from the rules	Come from the management and are in line with the work	Are created together	Arise alongside the meaningfulness of the work
Goals	Defined by the leader	Come from the organizational chart or a person with an such status	Are a measurement of success, defined by others	Sometimes one may set one's own goals, but usually set by one's supervisor	Are decided upon together
Directing operations	Where the boss wants to take them	Has been written down in the rules	Follows the vision of the director	Are set by management	Functions as basis for the work

The division of leadership and tasks in different leadership cultures

In individual-centered i.e. coaching leadership the role of a supervisor is to guide, help, and enable. The person as supervisor must have expertise in methods, organization, emotional knowledge, and curiosity so as to be able to spar with the employees and teams.

When moving to the level of community-centered leadership i.e. Teal organization (Teal theory, https://www.reinventingorganizations.com/) discrete supervisor roles are not needed. Of course, there are more experienced people in Teal organizations and teams as well, who often take a leading or mentoring role. In time everyone in the organization adopts the necessary skills and practices. When new people join, they naturally receive guidance from others and learn the necessary skills to be able to manage in an organization with an autonomous leadership model.

Goals and the Direction of Operations
Setting goals is very important. Without goals it would be difficult to work.

If there aren't any experienced employees in the organization, setting goals might be neglected. Goals should be set, and ways of measuring should be created to follow-up on their implementation. Setting short- and long-term goals requires experience; therefore, in an individual-centered leadership culture the directing of and the responsibility for this topic is still handled by a supervisor. In a community-centered organization the personnel can set the goals.

The direction of operations i.e. the organization's vision (goal) and mission (meaning) often come from somewhere above. Background factors may be regulation and legal issues, such as who owns the organization and why the organization was created to begin with. The task of Oodi, the Helsinki City Library, is to lend books, and this is an operational direction given from above. That organization is a community-led organization, but the direction of operations cannot be influenced by the personnel. Otherwise Oodi would no longer be a library.

In companies the goals are set by the owners. The company was founded for a business purpose. The owners may be committed to autonomous leadership and community-led methods, but they do not want to change the company's sector of industry, or at the very least they do not want to give the personnel the power to change it. In some cases the owners are so committed that they take personnel along into the management work so they can influence the business solutions of the company. In some companies shares in the company are sold to the employees, in which case it is very reasonable to allow the personnel to influence the direction of operations.

Mankind is developing constantly. The table on different leadership cultures presented above is just a visualized simplification of the different ways communities are led. In shared leadership it is possible to go over the borders of the table in either direction. The only thing permanent is the constant and ever-faster change.

Thanks to shared leadership organizations can react quickly to changes and give people the leadership that they desire – because every person is part of the leadership. The future is an ever-moving target which cannot be hit with fixed structures.

6.2 Responsibilities

In shared leadership one must be careful with sharing responsibilities. It is not worth defining the responsibilities too exactly. If a given task belong to someone else's responsibility, others will not take responsibility for it.

When people move about in places where there are cleaners, they easily throw rubbish on the ground. When people move about in places where there are no cleaners, they clean up after themselves. Why is that?

The bearing responsibility in shared leadership is based on that same subconscious activity. When one person takes on the responsibility for a task, the others might no longer necessarily take on any responsibility for that task. Even if the responsibility is not defined, it is possible to end up in a situation where "Matt has always taken care of this matter." If Matt stops taking care of the task, the others soon notice how Matt's actions affected their work. The meaning of things often becomes visible when something is missing. Then the matter must be discussed together: who will take on the responsibility for that task?

When people get familiar with a culture of shared leadership, everyone will notice how others are taking responsibility for various matters around them. Now everybody learns to appreciate that Matt does task 1 and Tina does task 2, and instead of complaints, the people doing things get praise because the others understand that they do not have to take care of these tasks. When Matt and Tina take responsibility for these tasks and everyone knows it, the others may focus on their own tasks.

Do Not Take Away Responsibility and Power
If the organization is still training or trying out shared leadership, give power and responsibility to smaller units. If these units, departments, or teams make mistakes, let them correct those mistakes themselves.

If in this case the upper level takes back control and corrects the mistakes, returning responsibility back to those people will be difficult, as they know that they do not really have power nor responsibility. Their power can be taken away whenever someone higher-up wants to.

For example, Andy is given the responsibility for a project X. Andy makes a mistake, after which the supervisor or someone else immediately comes to follow Andy's actions, and takes the responsibility away or clears up the mess and puts out the fires. "Let me take care of this." After this they try to return the responsibility to Andy, but he will not take it back anymore. His experience tells him that the responsibility belongs to the supervisors whenever things don't go as the supervisors have imagined.

Sharing responsibility among the personnel demands persistence and possibly financial resources as well. Practicing it may very well, at least initially, put a strain on everyone's nerves. Each team or group needs time to find their own internal model of operation. In these situations the team needs to be able to ask for help when necessary. Similarly, the supervisors must be able to offer help and support in a solution-oriented way – without blaming or complaining. It is ultimately about the supervisor's selflessness in novel situations.

How to be unselfish?

- ✔ Let others speak, do not interrupt people.
- ✔ Ask for the opinions of others, even if you have already made your own decision. Also be ready to change your original decision.
- ✔ In a leadership role, let others speak first and only afterwards present your own wishes.
- ✔ Always be ready to change your own point of view if necessary.
- ✔ Give the others a chance to question your decision.
- ✔ Help when asked to, or say when you will be able to help.
- ✗ Never override others, even if you sometimes have to correct their mistakes.
- ✗ Do not embarrass people in front of others.
- ✗ Don't disgrace anyone, but rather give everyone a chance to improve their performance.
- ✗ Do not explain or diminish your responsibility for a matter when you get feedback. Accept the feedback, even if you might disagree.

How to act when the other is acting selfishly

- ✔ Ask why they act as they do. However, don't start to discuss the matter, as your aim is just to get an answer and make them her think about the issue.
- ✔ Collect material on selfish behavior. Write down issues, dates, and what happened.
- ✔ Formulate the material so that you describe what happened and how you felt. Be precise, don't accuse, speculate, nor speak on behalf of anyone else in these situations. Write down just the facts which the other person cannot deny.
- ✔ Verify from a third party whether they have understood the issue in the same way as you – so as not to be blind and merely see the situation from your own point of view.
- ✔ First bring the issue up privately, one-on-one. The more difficult the issue, the more private the method of communication: at the very least a phone call, but a meeting would be better.
- ✔ Make sure that you yourself are mentally and physically okay when you bring the issue up. Arrange a meeting, and ask the selfish person to reserve time for your conversation.

- ✔ *Present your case on the basis of facts without blaming. Describe what happened and how you felt.*
- ✔ *Let the other person explain their point of view.*
- ✔ *Direct the person to find a solution themselves and agree on how such situations could be avoided.*

It is important to learn to act according to the division of responsibilities. One's own actions are a good calling-card for what you expect from others. If you do not act responsibly and selflessly, it is hard to expect that from others. The same applies to good manners. Shared leadership requires personal growth from everyone. Taking on and sharing responsibility is maturity. Shared leadership is maturity in the work life.

6.3 Roles

There are no static, fixed roles in shared leadership. This does not mean that the roles do not exist.

Each person's role is shaped according to their experiences while working, or the roles can be agreed on at the beginning of the project. The roles change according to what task is being worked on and what one's previous relation to that task or project is. For example, each meeting has a responsible leader, and each project has a project manager. These are defined on a case-by-case basis, not based on people's titles.

At team meetings there is a team leader, whose duties rotate for each meeting. By rotating the role we get experience on each team member's leadership, and gradually the team's shared practices are take shape. Everybody understands the tasks and obligations of leading a meeting. For example, when you lead a meeting where the others are rambling on, you learn to stick to the topic in your own future turns to speak. When a colleague covers for you or makes concessions when something was left unfinished, your empathy towards others grows for when they make mistakes.

A Project and a Project

In a traditional project delivery organization there is a chain of project managers, workers, and salespeople. A salesperson sells services and projects. When the sales are completed, a project starts and the responsibility is transferred to a project manager. If the customer does not have a familiar project manager from before, the next available project manager is chosen, and they then collect a team from the available workers and start the project. A lot of work time is used to exchange information to make sure that everyone involved have clearly understood what the customer wants and needs. Time is also used for familiarization with the subject at hand.

In a project organization utilizing shared leadership the operations are more agile. In completely autonomous community-led organizations there are no salespeople nor project managers at all. Everyone is a consultant, or more familiarly expressed, workers/doers. When a person sells work to a customer, they also carry it out themselves. If there is so much work that they cannot do it alone, they will ask their colleagues for help. In this case the person in question first acts in the role of salesperson and then in
the role of project manager.

The same person may also help out with another project, during which they act in the role of a worker. They may also function in the HR and marketing groups of the organization, for which they have those roles as well.

This is not possible in all organizations due to legal reasons, the nature of the work, or the goals of the organization. Nevertheless, shared leadership means that people seek out tasks which interest them. If there is too much workload or their interest fades, the person may leave the marketing group and just focus on their existing roles.

How Is It Elsewhere?
The same practices can be applied in many fields. Tasks based on titles are dismantled, and the existing responsibilities and tasks are surveyed. It is then evaluated whether groupings emerge, or whether tasks and responsibilities are kept discrete. It is not necessary to dismantle everything at once: it is possible to lightly start from smaller units and then continue from there.

What About Unpredictable Tasks, e.g. Customer Service?
It is hard to foresee how much time to reserve for unpredictable tasks. Some people want to focus on one role and to do just one task. In a service-based organization the production or expert duties of a person suffer if they are required to take care of customer service at the same time. Constant interruptions cut off productive work that requires concentration. In shared leadership it is not about being like an entrepreneur i.e. doing everything at

the same time and answering the phone as well. It is possible to agree on turns for customer service, so that expertise work can be
done without interruptions.

**Employees with Less Work Experience Often Want to Do Just Their Own Work, While More Experienced Veterans Want to
Do Something Else As Well**
This seems often to be the case, as more experienced workers understand the whole picture, and want to avoid wastage.

Reducing wastage, i.e. unproductive operations, is familiar from the Lean model, which was launched in the 1990's in the industry of Toyota. Waste is considered e.g. a worker waiting for materials and instructions, more products than needed being produced just in case, and time being spent on moving things around and looking for things as well as correcting mistakes. Wastage is also not utilizing the know-how of the personnel. An experienced worker often sees what kind of zipping up would minimize wastage and idling. They might for instance want to take part in not just producing a product, but also in selling it, thus saving time on having to explain to the producers what has been agreed on with the customer.

On the other hand, certain types of people may want to focus on just one role, regardless of the length of their career. This is also possible in shared leadership, as long as the work group agrees among themselves on the roles and everyone has stated their own wishes. Not all tasks need to be shared equally. If only two people are interested in selling and the others are not, why force the others to do that?

What about the "Crap Duties"?
There are always unpleasant roles or tasks. When someone does not want to take on a role, those tasks can be taken care of with a rotating turn order. In the process criteria are created to check that tasks are performed acceptably. If someone shirks their duties, they also have to do the next turn of that duty. If someone completely refuses to perform a given role, it should be discussed and agreed on whether that person can be exempted from that role entirely.

Sometimes a person with specialized skills which the others do not have leaves the organization. If nobody wants to learn this know-how, it is necessary to consider hiring a new person. If the level of autonomous leadership is high enough that community decides about hiring, it may sometimes be necessary to consider paying a higher salary to somebody.

Take sales work for instance. Not everyone wants to do it, nor do they know how to do it. The operations of organizations usually stops, however, if there are no customers. The people in the organization may be the top experts in their fields, but without sales there is no work for anyone and the company cannot afford to pay salaries. In this case the company's community-led personnel may have to decide to hire a salesperson at a high salary, as it's a matter of the common good.

In shared leadership it is sometimes necessary due to force of circumstance to fix roles or outsource things. The aim is, however, to offer everyone a chance to choose role that pleases them.

Not having titles is also a challenge to career development, as traditionally titles, responsibilities, and roles develop as the career advances. We are living in a transitionary period where the person's expertise and professional skills should be inferable from other things than just their past work roles.

6.4 Measuring Well-Being

In shared leadership the well-being and feelings of people should be measured often and regularly. It is important to quickly gain knowledge about whether the motivation or occupational well-being of the personnel is deteriorating. The measuring should however be light and easy, so that the personnel agree to participate in them often and feel that they are beneficial.

The most typical means are questionnaires carried out via various IT solutions.

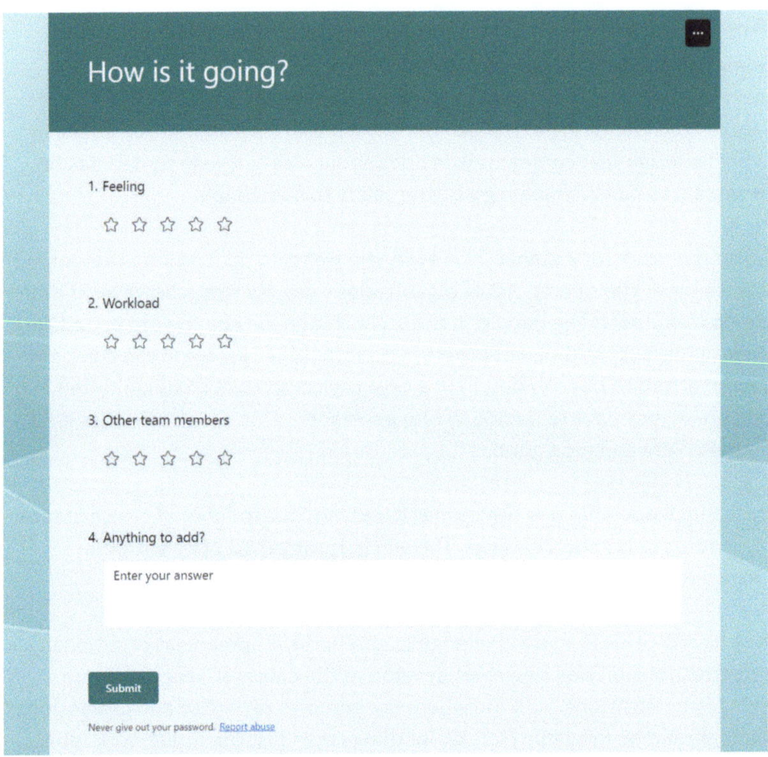

An example of measuring the feeling in a team or an organization

The picture above presents a type of light measuring of the overall feeling, which can be filled in in less than a minute. The questionnaire is sent out once a week to the personnel of the organization, and everyone is expected to answer it. The teams will then go through the results weekly at the team meetings. If a dip is noticed, even half a star in the mean value, the matter will be taken up and discussed to see what the reason is.

In a more traditional model, the satisfaction of the personnel is deduced occasionally with long questionnaires. Through this you can get some sort of idea about the situation in the organization. By measuring often and lightly you can follow the development of well-being and understand how vacations and the events of the surrounding world influence
the personnel's well-being.

The organization needs to decide on that itself, but often the task of creating and managing the questionnaire is given to the team responsible for human resources, i.e. the HR team. Each team itself is then responsible for their own team's results and the follow-up of those results.

Usually someone from the HR team carries the responsibility of it and takes on the task to follow the results of the other teams and their mean values as well. If a given team sees dips for several weeks on end, a representative of the HR team may contact them to ask whether they need help with the ambience or some other matter that needs to be improved.

The HR team may ask for external help, train itself or the organization's personnel if necessary. The HR team works like that of a traditional organization, the only difference being that the team is often comprised of consultants who work with other matters than just HR as well.

The measuring and follow-up of the personnel's well-being have a high priority in a shared leadership organization.

6.5 A Culture of Thanking

A Culture of Thanking Means Systematically Giving Positive Feedback.

A member of the community should show that they notice things in the environment. In shared leadership everyone takes a stand on matters happening around them, especially those influencing their own work.

In Finland there is no proper culture for giving feedback. However, the culture of thanking is an effective means to increase everyone's motivation and workplace satisfaction. In the culture of thanking, people regularly tell coworkers how their ways of working are felt in a positive way.

In a culture of thanking others are praised for the work they've done and other heart-warming deeds. It is not relevant whether the task in question was a responsibility of the person or not. People are thanked for the good feeling caused by their work and the relief to one's own work. Thanking can also be done in the presence of others.

Thanking is a small gesture but it means a lot to its recipient. When being thanked for your work every now and then, your work motivation and work satisfaction increase.

The culture of thanking can be applied to the whole organization as well as in smaller teams. A channel of communication can be created in the organization where anyone can thank anyone for their work. In teams and project groups it is recommended to reserve a portion of the weekly meetings for the culture of thanking. Usually people include the thanking in their own turn to speak, where they go over the tasks of the past week. At the same time it is a good opportunity to thank everyone who have contributed to finishing the tasks.

Tips on Giving Feedback

Often the selfish people in communities get thanks and the unselfish people get criticism. When an inflexible person who usually makes the work more difficult for others finally gives in to others, they get praise, which in itself is not wrong. However, the person who is usually flexible and covers for the others does not get thanks, but instead gets the blame for the rare occasion when they aren't flexible. Unfortunately often the frustration caused by a difficult person is taken out on those who do not put up a fight.

Take care that especially those who are constantly flexible and helping others get the thanks they deserve, and that their flexibility is not taken for granted nor as an obligation. Thank them not only for exceptional tasks, but also for their daily work.

- ✔ *Before a meeting reserve 5-15 minutes of time for yourself.*
- ✔ *Go through in your mind all the participants of the meeting.*
- ✔ *Make a list of everything you know they have done since the previous meeting. Use a calendar or task list to help you.*
- ✔ *Write down the positive or neutral matters.*
- ✔ *If some negative matters appear on the list, consider whether it is possible to give constructive feedback regarding them. If those matters are minor, get back to them later one-on-one. Consider whether it is necessary to give any feedback at all on the matters in question.*
- ✔ *When it is your turn to speak at the meeting, go through your list – praise and thank others.*

You may also share this feedback and these thanks whenever you meet the people in question. It is not wrong to thank twice, and it is also not wrong to thank for work well done or just in general for the person being there. Everyone gets happy when they are noticed and supported at work and elsewhere. Usually, the small things matter and give an extra boost for the day. However, do not give artificial or exaggerated thanks. A short thanking is efficient, and it will be remembered, even if took just a few seconds. We often take the work of others for granted and only notice the mistakes, but by learning to notice the good we end up seeing the things that work well instead of the mistakes.

6.6 Decision-Making

In shared leadership decisions can be made in various ways. The most important thing is to agree beforehand on in which situations and on which matters a given way of decision-making is to be used. Who will begin making decisions, and how quickly must the decisions be made? It is also good to set limits which areas each person can make decisions in, and whether they should belong to the relevant team for that area. Is it necessary to have the team's approval, or how do you ask for advice from others?

The following table presents different ways of decision-making. One-way declaration is the traditional way of a supervisor, which can be used in shared leadership as well when dealing with matters of one's own expertise or responsibility. That person may, for instance, have taken on the marketing duties of a start-up company when nobody else wanted to. In that case they may just announce to others how external communication is dealt with, and this policy is to be followed by the others as well. If there are disputes over the matter, the creation of a marketing team should be considered, and the manner of decision-making should be revised and agreed on.

	A one-way declaration procedure	An advisory process & Consultative decision-making	Democracy	Approval & Veto	Consensus
The method of decision-making	The traditional decision-making, where decisions are made by one person independently (often based only on their own point of view)	A decision may be made after consulting the people the decision relates to and those who know the most about the matter in question (a representative number of them)	Traditional democratic decision-making process, which warrants at least 50 % support for a decision	A decision can be made, if nobody actively objects to it or uses their veto right (passive approval)	A decision can be made once everyone thinks the suggestion is good (active approval)
The authoritarian version	The traditional boss attitude	Employees are consulted before deciding on matters relating to them	Partly giving in to democratic decision-making, but delineating in an authoritarian manner what can be decided on democratically and what cannot	Partly giving in to acceptance-based decision-making, but delineating in an authoritarian manner what matters can be decided on "together" and what cannot	Partly giving in to the consensus of the community, but delineating in an authoritarian manner what matters can be decided on "together" and what cannot
The communty-led version	Everyone is allowed to boss others around when it is about their own field of expertise, a so-called "meritocracy with blinders"	All members of the community may make decisions, as long as they follow the advisory process	Anyone can bring forth and prepare decisions to be made together	Anyone can bring forth and prepare decisions to be made together	Anyone can bring forth and prepare decisions to be made together
Assumptions	The decision-maker knows the best based on their position or expertise	An objective "correct decision" exists, which can be found out by asking for the views of colleagues	The normative assumption about the benefits of democratic decision-making	The non-manipulative usage of veto	Consensus does not dilute the decisions into futility

Various models for decision-making. Source: Haaga-Helia's publication 03/2021: Matkaopas yhteisöohjautuvuuteen, page 81

An advisory process & Consultative decision-making way, more familiarly known as an advisory process, is a general way to make decisions in community-led organizations. During it, those affected by the decision are consulted regarding it. Decisions are made according to certain rules and certain processes. In this model someone else makes the decisions that concern your work, and they then ask for your opinion. If you want your opinion to have weight, also give weight to others' opinions when you are making decisions.

Democracy is a familiar form of decision-making when dealing with decisions which feel important. Sometimes the venue of the organization's summer party gathers more opinions than strategic business decisions. In this case it is good to organize a poll to collect the votes of everyone willing, and then make a decision according to the majority.

The Approval & Veto process can be agreed to be used in certain areas, such as travel costs and the acquisition of tools. All invoices are open to everyone, and there is no reason to construct an approval process. When someone is making a sizable purchase in their opinion, a channel can be agreed on by which to inform about it. If nobody opposes or reacts to it, then anyone can decide on a purchase.

The consensus method of decision-making exists in teams quite naturally. Part of the team supports an issue and receives the support of the rest of the team. Agile teams find it impossible to define a separate method of decision-making for every situation, and then consensus i.e. discussions at meetings or on the team's communication channel is enough. Consensus comes naturally in those situations where there is no beforehand agreed-upon method of decision-making. If someone objects, one may need to shift over to an approval-based or democratic way of decision-making.

6.7 Processes

The same thing needs to be told to the same people again and again! Don't they ever learn? Part of these matters have always been dealt with as before - don't they remember that? It is so frustrating when people cannot think for themselves and solve problems. One needs to constantly give advice and check up on them. Actually, the problem is that they do not come to me with questions when there are problems. Whatever should I do in this situation?

When a person has had their tasks handed to them their whole career, it is hard for them to understand and take in that now it is time to think for yourself. The change does not happen overnight. In these situations one step at a time is taken so as to awaken the person to how to function in the future. Let them initially work on easier things independently, and later on more difficult things, so that their self-directedness begins to grow. When there are agreed-upon models of operation in the organization, these models help people to act in the right way and to understand the limits within which it is safe to make decisions.

When shared leadership is taken into use, it initially takes a lot of time for discussion, planning, and experimentation. The organization will gradually find a suitable way and suitable practices, which are then written down e.g. as a document. This document could be called the culture manual. It has all the instructions, advice, and practices which have been agreed on to be used in that organization.

The culture manuals of some organizations are public for the sake of transparency and for boosting the employer profile. Then the culture of transparency is emphasized and the same is also encouraged in the projects within the organization. Not everything needs to be published, only the main guidelines and principles. A process is commonly acceptable and valuable when it can be revealed to outsiders.

How to Begin to Plan Processes?

List the responsibilities

- *Does the organization have listed, what the responsibilities of different people, teams, or functions are?*
- *Do the projects have the responsible entities noted?*
- *Does the division of responsibility vary between different projects?*
- *Which responsibilities have been inherited? "It has always been done this way."*

List the rules of the game

- *What kind of rules does the organization have?*
- *What kind of rules is the organization lacking?*
- *What kind of rules are needed or requested?*

For instance, how to begin planning the processes of shared leadership from the point of view of the supervisor:

1. *Consider with whom to undo the old roles*
2. *Consider with whom to ponder the rules*
3. *State openly that you have recognized the problems*

4. *Ask who wants to take part in solving the problems*

5. *Try to motivate the people you desire to join the development*

6. *Organize a meeting where you bring the problems to the table and you together ponder solutions*

7. *Navigate the discussion, make notes, and guide people*

8. *Go through the results of the meeting and check whether any solutions came up that you had not thought of yourself*

9. *Ask the participants about their opinion on how to implement the matters discussed in the meeting*

10. *Make the roles, responsibilities, and rules visible:*

    - *mention them, and reinforce understanding when the topic comes up*

    - *print and post on the wall or in another way distribute to the personnel the info about what the roles, responsibilities and rules are*

    - *remember to be patient, these things need to be repeated often*

    - *be open to suggestions for change*

11. *Collect the problems that are still unsolved, and repeat the steps for a solution*

The process descriptions should not be long and cryptic documents, but clearly written and visual directions and advice. Draw pictures and charts.

When planning and forming processes it is also worth remembering the meaning of a culture of experimentation. Be open and try new ideas. Agree on roles of responsibility, i.e. does responsibility belong to certain people or does the responsibility rotate. The descriptions should always be up-to-date.

The processes of shared leadership are free when working in an individual- or community-centered culture of leadership. In an organization-centered culture everything is defined, even to smallest detail, but in shared leadership it is enough to document the big picture.

In shared leadership practicality and a human-centered approach are emphasized, not complex processes. Processes are however needed, in order to not have to reinvent the wheel every time.

7 CONCLUSION

In shared leadership there isn't the problem of the traditional organization, where a named director orders others around. The leader of a supervisor-led team needs to be able to take others into consideration. In a team without a supervisor, a bossy member of the team won't keep their status for very long, because the other members can vote with their feet. Everyone should be able to take the other members and their feelings into consideration.

On the other hand, there are various kinds of leader roles within the groups. All group members take responsibility and leadership in different situations, even if one person had a more dominant role than the others. Taking responsibility is also thanked, and is not taken for granted. A community-led culture teaches us to appreciate each other and the work we have done.

Selflessness and an impartial ability to observe matters are important qualities. In addition to this, everyone should be helpful and cooperative. With this combination it is possible to manage almost any situation. If a person is not automatically impartial, selfless, and helpful, these are skills that can be learned.

The first step is always to acknowledge and admit the problem or the challenging situation. If the organization's personnel do not understand or see the problems, they cannot be helped. For this reason, the organization and the teams within it need to be able to reflect on their own actions. A continuous measuring of the well-being helps in bringing forth situations where the personnel's motivation is deteriorating.

In shared leadership everyone has learned to give feedback, especially when someone is acting selfishly. The hardest is when a person does not accept the feedback and continues to act as before. In these situations, a one-to-one discussion is first held, and then within a small group, where two experienced people explain what is working well and what needs to be improved in the cooperation of the person in question.

To generalize, it could be said that in Finnish culture giving and receiving feedback requires training. There are a lot of instructions on giving constructive feedback. However, it is easier to adopt a culture of thanking, and it can be rooted from the start as a part of the operations of the organization. Initially it may feel a bit forced or even amusing to thank people for normal things. However, it develops into a habit which will contribute to well-being and compassion.

Nowadays most adults are able to make decisions together, no leaders are required anymore to make decisions on behalf of the personnel. On the other hand, it is important to agree on limits and methods of making decisions. Matters decided on together are noted into the process charts of the organization and are kept up-to-date.

Hopefully this book has been useful to you and you had important insights. Changing habits is a long and challenging road, but there is light at the end of the tunnel – as it is usually said. When an organization adopts shared leadership, it is truly possible to talk about a dignified work life.